Palace of Dreams

Peter Strawhan

Palace of Dreams

Selected Poems 1973–2012

Palace of Dreams: Selected Poems 1973–2012
ISBN 978 1 74027 817 1
Copyright © text Peter Strawhan 2013

First published 2013
Reprinted 2016

GINNINDERRA PRESS
PO Box 3461 Port Adelaide SA 5015
www.ginninderrapress.com.au

Contents

The pensioners	7
Matilda	8
The return of friends	9
Brooklyn Park	10
Now Time	11
Today	12
Ode to Xmas	13
Ode to Mortein	14
Machine Age	15
Roof-clutchers	16
TT Race	17
Travelling Companion	19
Medusa	20
Morning Journey	21
Roonka	22
Picture Me at the Exhibition	24
King Car	25
Life	26
Palace of Dreams	27
Left Bank Afternoon	28
Terra Australis	29
On Marriage	30
Queensland Journey	31
Communication	33
Parental Guidance	34
In Durance Vile	35
A Solitary Death	36
Lunchtime in Hyde Park	37
Hyde Park Paper Chase	38
Bird in the Park	39
Martin Place	40
Thoughts on the morning bus I	41
Thoughts on the morning bus II	42

Carla Zampatti	43
Blinman	44
Thoughts in the Bonython	45
Whale bones at the museum	46
Nearing the end of the road	47
Parting	48
Ficus Elephantus	49
Adelaide Airport	50
Ashford	51
On Survival	52
North Adelaide	53
Apologia	54
Smart-arse Society	55
Another Import	56
NZ Arrival	57
Beware	58
While Travelling Overseas	59
Morning Stroll	60
On not finding the Air New Zealand counter	61
Ponsonby Parade	62
Politick ticking away	63
Acceptance	64
Melbourne Terminal	65
Time Out	66
Autumn Morning	67
The New House	68
And Yet More	69
Walking Meditation	70
Whiteman's Dreaming	71
And Still We Shop	72
Pandora's Box	73
Return to Middleton	74
On the Cappuccino Coast	75
Larkin and Me	76
Flybys	77

The pensioners

They sit
Silent in the lowering gloom
Glazed eyes fixed
On the shimmering screen
Wrapped
In their own small grey cocoon
Surrounded
By the accumulation of the wasted years
Content
In their not knowing

Matilda

A sudden bark
Cleaves
The turgid night
Awake
In fright
Heart pounding
Mind snatched
From the far edge
Of sleep
Who let
The bloody
Dog out?

The return of friends

O frabjous day! Kaloo! Kalay
The prodigals are returning soon
To brighten up our days
No more they'll hear the merry clink
Of bottles near the Todd
The oft cursed canine chorus stilled
Along with 'bloody Abo sod'
No dainty sidesteps necessary to clear
The brawling boasters (just a wary eye
On dear old maids who drive like
Roller-coasters)
No atavistic prickling hairs to spoil
The evening saunter
Where via footbridge narrow across a stream
The dark-faced foemen gathered
But time flies quickly and tempers all remembrance
Till only rose-pink dawns remain
And harsh realities ended

Brooklyn Park

Dark fragmented memories come jostling from the past
Like black swans milling on muddy yellow waters
The stream of time jostling and pushing
Circling but not meeting in my mind
Damp and lonely sleepout
Sagging tar paper ceiling
Sickly roast on Sundays
Mustn't vomit control control
Wash down with milky tea
Nothing's wrong rissoles Monday
Sunday school good for the soul
Fire and brimstone preached
By the clean and colourless
Climb the platform it's God's anniversary
God! Who? Don't think
Mustn't think that in God's house
What's it mean?
There! No lightning bolt
Habit all habit no don't question
No don't think
What? Nothing nothing

Now Time

Time to lift the pennies from dead eyes
Time to see again the wild birds fly
Time to catch the sunlight's rays
Shining through the leaf-hung sky
Time to walk homeward through the gentle rain
Time to cast a pebble in to the stream
Time to watch the ripples widen
Until the sky darkens with my dreams
And all is still and all is still

Today

No warmth in our souls
No fire in our bellies
Complaisant acceptance
Of the norm our lot
The lowest common denominator
Controls our destiny

Ode to Xmas

Plastic Xmas with plastic snow
For plastic people with no place to go
Plastic fat men in sticky red suits
With plastic toys for the good little boys
Plastic signs to point the way
To plastic towns under lead filled skies
Plastic people in their plastic clothes
Too burdened with pleasure to know their pain
Plastic prayers for a long dead God
From plastic priests without a flock
Plastic cars and plastic trains
For plastic people with their futile aims
Plastic life and plastic death
With push-button flames
To finish the mess

Ode to Mortein

What fiend in hell devised the fly?
That degrading ultimate obscenity of life
How could the great and noble Christ
Have been a party to its foul design?
Black and ugly busy harbinger of disease
Corrupt product of dung heaps foul
How can this vast continent of ours
Play host to such abysmally evil things?
What irony that these sparkling skies
Unleash such clouds of this devil's device

Machine Age

Angry people encapsulated in glass and steel
Rigidly observing the demarcation lines of challenge
Their patch by divine right not of conquest
But to be defended at all costs with belligerence
The hallowed machine only must not be sullied
Unless challenge met with challenge results
In contact ugly scrape and bang of steel on steel
Rend of fabric and shatter of glass satisfies
Momentarily and then quick remorse not for
The injured but only for the machine
The hallowed phallic substitute

Roof-clutchers

Another strange antipodean curiosity
I see them often in my daily grind
They seem to have become more numerous of late
Even noticed one tonight threading through
Traffic islands with contemptuous ease
Largish boat in tow behind familiar Holden
Hairy right arm at right angle through
The open window hand clasping turret top
In possessive curlicues of righteousness
Rather like those weird crabs that grow
One huge claw to attract the female
Of the species I wonder if the roof-clutcher
In time will develop in similar fashion?
Perhaps the reason for the breed is clearer now
See my hairy arm protect the machine
So too I could encompass your slim shape
In my embrace or is it a challenge for all
To see a gauntlet of flesh to be thrown away
When Holden collides with Ford or Jap
And rough bitumen abrades skin from bone
As the metallic cocoons perform their final
Ritualistic pirouettes of death

First published in *Old Bike Australasia*, January 2013

TT Race

Two men with their machines
Pitted against the mountain course
Protagonists Mike and Alex
The bets are on
Grunt and heave patter of feet
They roar away screaming fours
Down Bray Hill and off through
The bends and swerves
Town and village echoes and re-echoes
The glorious sound of multi-cylinders
Raised in anger through Braddan
On and on
Leap through space at Ballaugh
Flat out through the gears
Streaming up the mountain
Into the drifting mists of Snaefell
Split seconds apart Mike leads
On the road but it's Alex on time
Each striving to win
As lap follows lap
All too soon time runs out
But for whom? It's Alex leading
At the Bungalow the fans go wild
How impossible it seems
Two men on such disparate machines
Can yet be so evenly paired
Tied by an invisible string
Riders matching move for move
Down Bray Hill they flash
The Scot ahead takes the chequered flag

The Castrol god defeated but Hailwood
The leather clad idol still
Has secured his place in history
And tamed the mountain circuit
Mile upon speeding mile

Travelling Companion

Eh? Eh? Fuckin' bewdiful Peter
Init? Init? Eh? Eh?
I seen this fuckin' thing yesterdee
Fuckin' nice it was y'know bluddy
Bewdiful eh? Get onto the fuckin'
Boobs on that fuckin' 'ell!
That wouldn't be fuckin' right would it?
On the other and it could be you might
Be fuckin' right but then agen –
Belch 'scuse a pig-fart fart
Silence – belch 'scuse a pig
Eh? Peter Peter wot a cunt of a place
Init eh? Init? No fuckin' 'ot water
A-fuckin'-gen. Eh? Eh?

Medusa

Dreadful old woman sits waiting
For the London train clawing
Strawberries from a crumpled brown
Paper bag devouring the ripe fruit
She drops the stalks at her feet
Along with the unsound rejects
Lights up another cigarette chin cupped
With the same hand that holds
The weed in continuous motion
She sucks and puffs sucks and puffs
Devouring the cigarette as she devoured
The fruit mouthing the smoke
In to the gaping cavern of her face
Beneath the rumpled wide-brimmed hat
The tendrils wreath around the decayed
Medusa she so well personifies

Morning Journey

Poor dead bird
Lying by the roadside
Like a pair of feathered
Hands joined in supplication
A brief prayer perhaps
To a benign and merciful God?
Or a muted protest
With no roll of drums
To the mechanical omnipotent
Who now holds sway over all
Our frenzied journeying

Roonka

Dead gum trees stark
Against the morning sky
The early mists just recently
Departed had wreathed their grey
Tendrils lovingly around the silvered
Trunks the high cliffs touched
With pink from the quickly rising
Sun give shelter to the living
And the dead the living from myriad
Points of vantage soar and glide
Riding the invisible thermals
With avian grace the long dead
Fossils banded in countless numbers
Slumber on not caring
Down on the flat we toil carefully
With brush and trowel removing
The encrusted sand from the smaller
Skeleton disturbing the accumulated
Covering of the centuries
Could this pitiful collection once
Have housed a soul a mind?
And if a soul where does
The spirit wander? Will our
Uncovering of its bones cause
Further suffering? Surely one
Short span was toil enough

With the child removed the female
Lay exposed as perchance she lay
For the huntsman not under the hot
Sun now burning our backs and limbs
But later in the cool darkness
The same myriad stars
On their southern pilgrimage
Must have witnessed their
Lovemaking the rustling
Night sounds damping out their
Moans of pleasure as the
Cooking fires died one by one
And only the ghostly river gums
Stood sentinel like spirits
From the dreaming

Picture Me at the Exhibition

A sense of not belonging
Anywhere
Total detachment
From the whole of being
Like a single dried-up pea
Rattling in an empty pod
Not part
Of any scene or even
Any scheme
Of things
Past present or future
No umbilical cord
Supports my being
The life juice flows
In vacuum

King Car

Serried ranks jockeying
For position storming
From intersection to intersection
From green go to red whoa
The puppets respond
To the invisible puppeteers
Hidden in the omniscient
Metal boxes
Common sense with consideration
Vanished people no longer matter
The car is king
We change behind the wheel
Of the magic car car
The futility of the exercise
Is lost on all of us
As each meaningless journey
Joins the next
And the myriad streams
Criss and cross while
The unseeing eyes
Blink their commands
The saliva drips and Pavlov preens

Life

Cul-de-sacs predominate
In the labyrinth of life
No rigid line connects
The cradle to the grave
A tenuous thread finds
The waiting Minotaur
For all of us
But on the way
We back and fill
Quite a good deal

Palace of Dreams

The brown beanbag
Lies dishevelled
At the foot of the stairs
Effectively blocking access
To the palace of dreams
Atop the flight
Turn right at Leonardo
To transports of delight
A neat gymnastic trick
To clear the barricade
But to no avail
The prerequisite cannot
Be met no casual
Peccadillo will suffice
To overcome your virtuous
Forbearance only the favoured
One it seems
May pass behind

Left Bank Afternoon

Wild weather afternoon
After the fretful morning
Dust the autumn leaves
Toss in the gusty wind
High against the city greyness
Suddenly the rain comes
Driving down the air sweetens
As the staccato pattern begins
Droplets run down the window
Making rivers in the grime
At last the long summer ends

Terra Australis

Anzac the myth long since exposed
Lies central to our genesis
Almost a nation but never quite
The chance the burning torch not grasped
Deceived by our leaders then as now
Innocents abroad sacrificed like drought-
Stricken roos first herded then shot down
Against the fences of Gallipoli and Flanders
The simple-minded acceptance of the role
Denies all logic and yet we continue
To clutch the straw of dependence
On the arbiters of Washington as once
Westminster reluctant to come of age
To come to terms with the here and now
So many negatives combine to shape the frame
Of our collective being the sunlight glinting
On the lonely iron roofs outback
Reminder of hapless searchers after inland seas
Where now the bulldozed carcass of the Dreamtime
Lies raped by insatiable greed for instant wealth
The clay pans spread and the salted streams
Blacken the vines while our cities sprawl
Under the grey pall of conservatism and mediocrity
Mingled with their filth carefully decanted
Into once clear azure skies

On Marriage

You drain me
Suck the life force
From me
Now only the shell
Bitter remnant remains
To prop up the myth
Of caring
Of continuing
You leech-like
Surround me
Constantly devouring
Draining away the sap
The husk stands
For the time

Queensland Journey

The corpses litter the roadway
For a thousand miles or more
Lying with obscene abandon
Their bloated guts fine pickings
For the black-suited undertaker crows
Waiting until the last second
They fly heavily away
From each passing car
Quickly returning to a new vantage point
The better to prod and tear red flesh
And glistening white sinew
Pulling the strands apart
No hope of resurrection left here
Kangaroos reddish brown or grey
Large and small caught like frozen images
From some horror movie still
Twisted necks and broken limbs
The odd delicate paw lifted in vain protest
The national symbol how proud we are
Black faced fine limbed wallabies lie broken
Scattered dismembered foul the black ribbon
Stretches on and the numbers grow
From each shimmering horizon to the next
Here a swollen black pig looms
Uglier in death even than in life
Sharp teeth bared in the rictus of
Its final agony poor innocent stumpy tail
Lies nearby somehow selected to join the carnage
Banded round by black columns of ants

There another pathetic long-legged bundle
Once a loose striding feathered skirts flying emu
The list goes on and on throughout
The long drawn cheerless day
Until merciful night closes down the dismal scene
Only the miasma of death stays
In our nostrils lingering complement
To the mental images we cannot shrug away

Communication

I tried to talk to you
For years I tried but
The words would never come
Christ knows I tried
Not hard enough perhaps
Not often enough perhaps
But I'm sure I tried simple
Enough if you have the knack
If the ground is common
If the lines are open
Words should come should flow
Should explain the why the wherefore
The beginning and the end
But the tears came first wrenching
My guts my sobs wild unbidden
Broke the ice of silence
All of the pain and yes
All of the guilt flowed with my tears
Then the unreasoned mumblings
Turned at last to words
The banalities of convention
Came tumbling out not well not
Colouring not adding comfort to
The bare ribs of anguish not extinguishing
Either hurt not softening not soothing
Not changing anything not explaining
How can the unknown be explained?
But I did try I know I tried

Parental Guidance

If you won't stay at school
And make the most of your
Opportunity you must have
A trade son what's five years?
Not a bloody eternity feels like
One don't get smart with me
The motorcar is here to stay
So get stuck in and find the way
Cheap labour? Don't be dumb
You can't expect good money
While you learn the game
Fifteen bob a week? That's
More than I got when I was
Your age so sweep the floor
And get the lunches maybe
One day we'll let you fix
Some punctures never mind
That bullshit they teach at Trade
School there's only one way
To learn some skills and that's
To work not bloody shirk
What do you mean we should
Have more equipment use your
Back and your hands not the brains
In your head What, the hammer
Slipped? Wipe the tears and swear
Instead. It's do as I say not do
As I do you've got to learn
Your place if you want to stay
In the bloody race

In Durance Vile

I would hate to be huddled
In a tiny cottage with peeling
Wallpaper and salt damp
Rising inexorably like death
Upon the wall's ugly horizon
The smell of damp and decay
Clinging at nostril height
And the ever deepening
Ever determined silently ominous
Cracks appearing as if by
Some conjuror's aimless directive
The lifting rusted iron
Still managing to keep out rain
Apart from the odd trickle
Which somehow finds the already
Damp now clammy cold must
Perfumed pillow stripped
In disrepute its slip long gone

A Solitary Death

The tennis courts are empty
No games today because
Gentle Tim killed himself
Just that other day
After carefully attending
To his affairs he finalised
His life I only knew him briefly
Not long enough to know
His strife others who knew him
Longer better had no warning
Sure he was down but we all
Get depressed at people and events
The saddest thing is that his friends
Couldn't help if he did ask
Not one of us realised his need
A solitary deed to die
Like that unaided and alone

Lunchtime in Hyde Park

The green of the park
Offers some escape
From acidic traffic fumes
Frenetic pace and noise stilled
The autumn sun shines
And shafts through trees
Ibis wandering amongst the gulls
Hint of distant exotic climes
The noisy gulls allow
Their peaceful cousins space
But the imperative demands
Their own kind be driven off
Away from the crumbs
At our feet
In the sun of Hyde Park

Hyde Park Paper Chase

He looked like any other Sydney
Derelict this garbage collector
Surely a self-appointed scavenger
Towing his black plastic sheet astern
Hessian lined like some strange bulging
Carapace fierce of mien and determined
He ploughed across the lunch time lawns
Newly loaded the scraps of paper
Suddenly alive rebelled began escaping
From their roughly shaped confines
Quickly laid a paper chase
For holidaying children
Screaming curses the dero fell upon his knees
In rage he pummelled and shoved
Fighting the re-littered horde
Back back into its shrouded resting place
We aloof stared like the red-eyed seagulls
Waiting for our other scraps

Bird in the Park

A strange noise echoed through the park
We looked at each other eyebrows raised
What the hell was that?
Again and yes again it sounded
Then continued like some strange bird call
Played on a weird oriental instrument
Cross between what? Maybe baboon
And perhaps macaw who knows?
Then tripping down the pathway came
A well-groomed blonde
Shining hair tightly bunned
In the classical mode
She wore a mid-length white lacy
See-through dress with overtones
Of *Swan Lake* smiling sweetly all serene
Head thrown back mouth wide
And open she ululated her wild call to nature
With another series of barking shrieks
Somehow crossed through the midday
Maelstrom of Elizabeth Street
Without pausing and disappeared
Still briefly calling as she went
We may have been the only ones who noticed

Martin Place

The Flugelman tetrahedrons
Perch uneasily on their pyramid
Dwarfed by the respectability
Of the lighthouse-like clock tower
Against the evening sky
A crane presents its triangulated profile
Atop the endmost building
The myriads homeward bound
Look ahead or around
Perhaps they sense the danger
In looking up
Concrete and glass dwarf all
Unlikely trees thrust skyward
From bleak grey pavements
In the end they more fortunate
Will endure

Thoughts on the morning bus   I

Overnight the jacarandas have erupted
In their various shades of blue
Through the not-quite-clean
Window of the workday bus
They seem of infinitely variable hues
Especially to my mildly colour-blind eyes
Which by this distinction may not be quite
As jaundiced as their owner oft believes
The black pods thickly clustered
On that other tree hang
Like some inanimate colony of bats
But have an attraction of their own

Thoughts on the morning bus   II

Scraped clean
Dutifully presented
Daily
With a tinge of Brut
Mainly thankful
For the small mercy
Of the fortnightly
Payslip
But always one behind
Because inevitably
Consumerism
Takes the place
Of frugality

Carla Zampatti

Sipping a quick cappuccino
Across the mall
A tony upmarket boutique
For the trendies
White hats wide-brimmed
Broad and shiny black belts
Symbol of their own
Particular brand of prowess?
Broadly padded shoulders
De rigueur
As the fashion wheel whirls
Round and round
The circle of style decreases
An unlikely window-shopper stops
She is grotesque in pink
Shaped by her very own
Inbuilt bustle of flesh
A mammoth manikin
Past middle age maybe
Shopping for a sylphlike daughter
Or lost in her own fantasy
Of what might once have been

Blinman

Over the hill
Behind the bald black plateau
Of the slag heap
The wind is knife keen
But thankfully
The constant wearing hum
Of the diesel generator
Has disappeared
Like the hands
That disembowelled
The hillside
And left their mark
For another generation
Of despoilers
Who toil not
But litter well
On their way to view
The once sacred
They distribute plastic
Scraps from 4WDs
And dare to scratch
Their own meaningless
Initials among
Man's oldest symbols
But the black rocks
Are ever patient

Thoughts in the Bonython

It was most unsettling
During the Vivaldi
When the fly landed
On the silver head
Of the cardiganned gent
Nodding off on my left
My roving eye was busily
Assessing the erotic
Potential of the small Swiss
Blonde wielding her large violin
Under the left armpit
Of the leader
Having just decided
Her jaw was too rigid
By far – or was it
The shop assistant's
Downturn to the lips
The fly zoomed in
And settled into place
I shivered
It was as if the grave
Had yawned open at my feet
Or a maggot had popped
Out of Bray's left eye
Mind you – that would
Have been less a threat
More like a confirmation

Whale bones at the museum

Yesterday the whale bones were uplifting
My spirits soared at the sight of their immensity
That great vaulted dome sets the scale
For the whole logic defying structure
How? Why? The questioning began and since
Unanswerable today depresses me
Simply a collection of white painted objects
Part of a display mounted to assuage
The guilt in some small measure

Nearing the end of the road

The sparring continues
The ritual is unchanged
I'll have a last cigarette
You go along to bed
Dismissed
Like a naughty little boy
Brave boys don't cry
A chip off the old block
Why would he need to cry?

Parting

Snip!
The umbilical cord is severed
And just as soon the pain begins
Mind-numbing gut-wrenching
Bone crunching when will it end?
As if to say it has a mind
Of its own perhaps it has
But to teeter on the brink of the abyss
Cannot be borne for long
That other section of being
Must prevail must re-establish
Control to stop the hurt
And allow life again

Ficus Elephantus

Moreton Bays
Remind me of elephants
They are similarly folded
And wrinkled
Comforting
But with an air
Of no nonsense
Having been around
For a long time
And likely to remain
For a good many aeons
Longer than us

Adelaide Airport

I sit semi-patiently
Allowing more minutes
Of my life to tick
Wastefully by of course
The plane is late
The airport bar an inhospitable
Oasis the server predictably
And patently bored
Save when a friendly
Phone call effects a fleeting
Transformation the flagon red
Is drinkable but the price
Per glass ensures my sober
Reflection. 'Abby this is not
A playground.' from the black-
Panted two-toned and razor-cut
Young mum as her child swarms
Up the bar stool other children
Shriek I cut my losses by beating
A quick retreat the plane
Is still late

Ashford

The roses in the jar
Are quite beautiful
He also tended roses
In his time but now
Nearing the end
Of that all too brief
Allotted span instead
Drops ice cream on
His newly changed
Pyjama top we
Embarrassed look
Away and consign
Him to his lonely fate

On Survival

My mouth is dry
With the fear
Of being alone
I rely too heavily
On hearing your
Bright voice recount
The doings of your
Day knowing I can
Survive without you
But mere survival
Is not enough

North Adelaide

Black tracery of branches overhead
Cathedral spires in need of restoration
Stand mutely overseeing concrete
Building blocks close by the gargoyled
Pepper trees conjure bleak asphalted
School yards crisp frost touched air
Bites impartially at ears and fingers
While discarded leaves pretend to be
A forest floor but still confirm
The season's change then blasting
Horn and screeching tyres shatter
Morning's brief reverie white Porsche
Knight concedes apologetically
To black Ford and waves the victor on
With them the elusive muse departs
As eight chimes ring out to sound
The weekday's morning knell

Apologia

Congratulations!
You did it again
Breaking in
On someone else's
Stream of consciousness
It was too easy
After you plied your wares
Inserting yourself lubriciously
Between her covers
Disrupting the pattern
Of her life
How do you feel now?
When it's all over
The taste of her ashes
In your mouth

Smart-arse Society

It occurs to me
That we will never be
The clever country
While we remain
The smart arse society
Singleton Murdoch Packer et al.
Have seen to that
The big end of town
Their false world a cloud cuckoo land
Friends with money hype and bullshit
Maintaining the rageless ockerdom
Of that lowest common denominator
With whirling chocolate wheels
Of fortune selling off our century
With all their false promises

Another Import

The clever country?
In a pig's ear mate
Not with garlic from China
Dates from Israel
Walnuts from Turkey
Almonds from the good-ol' USA
Juice concentrate from Brazil
You name it betcha it's imported
Nuts packed in Australia
Big deal using local and
Wait for it imported products
We can't even get our regulations right
Gave up on tuna long ago
Read the small print feel you are
Being conned? Whatever gave you
That impression? Someone is being
Clever but it's not us
We emulate the ostrich another import

NZ Arrival

The lights of Auckland
Glowing below
Like fire walkers'
Red hot coals
A white man's dreaming
Whine of flaps
Thunk of undercarriage
Locking down into place
The starboard wing drops
A sudden scary forward surge
Then a settling back
A lone blinking light
Reflected at the wing tip
Full flaps and reverse thrust
Shuddering we go in
To abrupt black darkness

Beware

You skate precariously
On the thin ice of my feelings
Beware the cold depths beneath
I am rarely what I seem
Like those plastic strips
Hanging in doorways
I twist and turn
From moment to moment

While Travelling Overseas

After recent travails
I get busy
Repairing my defences
Like a spider
Mending its damaged web
How fragile
Are the gossamer ties
In this alien clime

Morning Stroll

The ever-changing river
In the light of early morning
Is a sheet of stippled glass
The vectoring pelicans
Silently patrol each unmarked claim
Aloof from their busy cousins
Among the reeds
Disturbed at my approach
The ibis cry out a warning
And clumsily take flight
Perhaps puzzled
By the absence of pyramids
Black-clad shags perch
With disdain on private jetties
Drying their wings after breakfast
A sailboat glides serenely in to view
The waking breeze catches hold
And the suddenly curving bow wave
Glistens in a shower of sunlight
The magic of the moment ends
With a speeding stink boat
The screaming outboard
Shatters the brief serenity as its
Creaming wake troughs out of sight
Spreading quickly shore-wards
Rocking the moored flotillas

On not finding the Air New Zealand counter

Like her late
Gracious majesty
We are not amused
The queue is long
So too the face
Of the customs officer
'Get thee hence'
She declaims
'And return here
With the correct
Boarding pass'
So much for safety
Nets of time
My margin for error
Dwindles rapidly
The salutary reminder
'You are on standby'
The computer is down
Saint Anthony
Where are you?

Ponsonby Parade

God created Adam
And Eve – not
Adam and Steve
So ran the limp banner
High on the scaffolding
Corseting like an iron maiden
That building in a state
Of resurrection
On Ponsonby Road
The morning after
Auckland's Parade of Heroes
Passed energetically by
With and without their finery
Lights lingering
Over thrusting buttocks
While torsos twisted
To the heavy beat
And whistles blew
Sounding trumps
The happy conjunction
Of truckies ferrying
Their varied cargoes
Just a touch surreal
But the crowded pavements
Approved
And we were among friends

Politick ticking away

In the fine flowering
Of his genius
Yeats decided the centre
Could no longer hold
Now both Labor and Liberal
Sit in that middle ground
While things around
Fall apart as you see
And as your children
Will find to their higher cost
But God must with a little help
From his friends
In their high places
Preserve all Dames and Knights
As a question of acute priority
'…and the times are hardening fast'*

---

* From 'A Tangential Death', Marge Piercy, *Stone, Paper, Knife*, Pandora, London 1987

Acceptance

Do not despair my friend
Somewhere
Along the way
Visions
Of immortality
Gently slip away
To be replaced
By quiet acceptance
Of a common destiny
Our brief flutter
Like the Wanderer
Butterfly
A mere blink
In the majesty
Of Earth's time

For Brian Callen; read at his funeral 12 December 1996

Melbourne Terminal

The Walkman, alas, is in my suitcase
A mindless cacophony permeates the building
Constant jarring repetition to my ear
The same strident beat washing over
The great unwashed words indistinguishable
From Muzak does anyone listen?
Does anyone care? How to endure
The unendurable electronic metronome
Hammering into our skulls
The talentless mouth obscenities
Of lurv in their high-pitched wails
Through the glass the land is silent
Under the grey mist

Time Out

The dunes were beyond time
Even as dew-wet branches
Slapped in passing
Our bare legs
Time begins
When we walk
Onto the beach
Gulls teased the dog
Just by their presence
And distant horses
Exercised ever closer
To my eye the sands
Glowed pink and gold
While sea mist
Curtained the far hills
Busy white-topped breakers
Dotted the blue ocean
Like so many
Snow-white handkerchiefs

Autumn Morning

Blue sky and bright sunshine
Herald approaching spring
A busking magpie
Carols skywards
From dew-soaked grass
But the August breeze
Still speaks
With an icy tongue
Along the empty wharf
Licking at discarded wrappers
Riffling yesterday's bunting
Still festooning
Deserted market stalls
On the boardwalk
Patches of frost
Match shadowed intervals
Cast by regimented posts
And lie in wait
For the unwary

The New House

This morning early
At the house
Upstairs I opened
The sliding doors
To let the fresh
Morning breeze stir
Through wafting away
That new-laid carpet smell
Four welcoming swallows
Already used to perching
On their back deck circled
Investigating our presence
The bravest or most foolhardy
Flew inside to check out
The new lie of their land
And satisfied with our intentions
Exited at centre stage
Without comment

And Yet More

Blown by the wayward
Winds of chance
I fetched up
On the lee shore
Of your soft bosom
Where I still lie
And hope to do thus
Until I die

Walking Meditation

Friendly old tree
Were you standing there
When I walked by
This morning? The path
Seems familiar surely
I'd have noticed
That welcoming stance
Like a benevolent stranger
One meets by chance
Is this not the path?
Or have conjunctions moved
In some mysterious way
To finally reward my day

Whiteman's Dreaming

Rest assured my friends
The river is safe in our hands
However it doesn't pay
To rush things
We'll appoint another
Expert committee
And await their report
Trust us
The Ngarrindjerri weep
The river slowly dies

And Still We Shop

Sculptured sardine cans
In all the colours of the rainbow
For all of us foolish little fishes
To slaver over as we swim
To the fresh-food people
Lining up dutifully in our
Designated positions then
Stocked up with bargains
Of the week: look two for only
Thirty dollars What a saving!
Let us rejoice as we jockey back
Upstream and green says GO!
No more the ceaseless tramp
Of feet now it's the remorseless roar
Of sardine cans glorying
In their triumph

Pandora's Box

During the cold war we worried
At the ever present threat of extermination
In the aftermath of nuclear fired confrontation
Between the two behemoths
As Neville Norway Shute described so well
So chillingly our world could become
The silence of the grave a silence
Broken only by the radioactive wind
Turning a creaking windmill
Until it too grinds to a halt
Instead only the sons and daughters
Of Bushido were strategically incinerated
With less fortunate thousands left alive
To share Madame Curie's lingering fate
The rest of us survived and limped
Into a fresh century
Hoping not to witness another such time
Of barbarism unequalled in its size
Though we should know too well
With Pandora's box yawning wide
Our pathway leads only to oblivion
Likely not with quick release
Of the almighty bang instead
The tortured drawn out suffering
Of barely heard whispering
From the billions of our kind
Swarming over the tired Earth
Until it cries enough enough

Return to Middleton

Walking early
On the still damp sand
Not long after sun up
Casts long shadows
Under brilliant blue sky
A distraction
From the main player
Ever changing
But unchanging
That Great Southern Ocean
Breaks and swells and breaks
Again and yet again
Maybe forever
In terms of our brief intrusion

On the Cappuccino Coast

Etched against the early morning sky
A long white vapour trail
Arrows towards Perth
The wintry sun climbs rapidly
From the eastern horizon
Scattering thin blue ribbons of cloud
Like a sudden starburst:
On the beach Jackie noses
In to a pile of freshly mounded seaweed
That serves to hide the ugly brown stains
Discolouring once pristine white sand
A few wet-suited board riders
Ignore cappuccino-coloured breakers
And paddle through toxic-looking sludge
In search of more wholesome waves
Further out beyond the point

Larkin and Me

Larkin largely drank himself
To death at 63
His Mum and Dad certainly
Fucked him up
Mainly his Mum
Who died at 91
Before her son
But all the damage
Long done
Mine on the other hand
Succumbed at 97
Missing out on the telegram
By a scant three years
While to my surprise
I somehow managed
To outlast her
This then is my conceit
Whatever does Larkin
Have to do with me?

Flybys

Outside the terminal
Rain spatters down
Glistening on white wings
And the long cylinders
They somehow support
Inside the systems maze
We approach our waiting
Allocated space shuffling
Along the long carpeted
Chambers isolating the within
From the without welcomed
On board by the leader
Of our lovely crew
Her unintelligible pronouncements
Preceded by the requisite three
Musical dongs – earlier alas!
My home-printed boarding pass
Lacking a barcode was rejected
But 'no problem' (that now ubiquitous
Phrase) since by some sleight of hand
The correct issue in my name
Lies waiting at the attendant's fingertips
Relief floods my aged brain
Trying to cope with all the manifest
Advantages wrought by ever smarter
Technology that has delivered us to
This wondrous paperless
Largely joyless society

www.ingramcontent.com/pod-product-compliance
Lightning Source LLC
Chambersburg PA
CBHW062151100526
44589CB00014B/1778